The BIG Stink

Jim Eldridge

Illustrated by
Tamara Anegon

OXFORD
UNIVERSITY PRESS

OXFORD
UNIVERSITY PRESS

Great Clarendon Street, Oxford, OX2 6DP,
United Kingdom

Oxford University Press is a department of the University of Oxford.
It furthers the University's objective of excellence in research, scholarship,
and education by publishing worldwide. Oxford is a registered trade mark of
Oxford University Press in the UK and in certain other countries

Text © Jim Eldridge 2017

Illustrations © Tamara Anegon 2017

The moral rights of the author have been asserted

First published 2017

All rights reserved. No part of this publication may be reproduced, stored
in a retrieval system, or transmitted, in any form or by any means, without
the prior permission in writing of Oxford University Press, or as expressly
permitted by law, by licence or under terms agreed with the appropriate
reprographics rights organization. Enquiries concerning reproduction outside
the scope of the above should be sent to the Rights Department, Oxford
University Press, at the address above.

You must not circulate this work in any other form
and you must impose this same condition on any acquirer

British Library Cataloguing in Publication Data
Data available

978-0-19-837755-9

9 10 8

Paper used in the production of this book is a natural, recyclable product
made from wood grown in sustainable forests. The manufacturing process
conforms to the environmental regulations of the country of origin.

Printed in China by Leo Paper Products Ltd.

Acknowledgements
Inside cover notes written by Karra McFarlane
Author photograph by George Carrick

Contents

1 The Case of the Disappearing Fish   5
2 Follow the Rats   14
3 The Big One   23
4 Escape by Smell   33
5 Spotted!   45
6 Home at Last   54
About the author   64

Chapter 1
The Case of the Disappearing Fish

"I've got us a case," said Cat.

"What sort of case?" asked Dog. "A suitcase? A bookcase?"

They were in the back garden of the house where Dog lived with Mrs Thing.

Mrs Thing was a kind woman but she was kept so busy with her work that she didn't have much time to spend with Dog. She made sure she put down a bowl of water and some biscuits for him every morning before she went off to work, and gave him a bowl of food every evening when she came home.

Dog was happy enough because during the day he hung around with Cat, a stray cat. Cat was his best friend.

"It's going to be our first case as *Cat and Dog Detectives*," said Cat. She produced a large card and fixed it to the front of the kennel. It said:

Cat and Dog Animal Detectives
If you are an animal and you've got a problem, come to us. No job too small.

Dog frowned.

"I didn't know we were going to be detectives," he said.

"Yes, you did," said Cat. "We talked about it last week. I suggested us being detectives, and you asked what detectives did."

"Yes," nodded Dog thoughtfully. "I did. I remember now."

"And I told you that detectives solve problems. They investigate things that are wrong and put them right. They do things like look for people and things that have gone missing. Or, if anyone steals anything, they find out who did it. I told you that's called detecting."

"Yes, you did," nodded Dog again. He looked at Cat. "So, what's this case you've got for us to detect?"

"*The Case of the Disappearing Fish,*" said Cat. "All the cats in town are worried about it. Someone is stealing all the fish from the shops and restaurants. Who's doing it? And why? Fish is a cat's favourite food. If we can solve this case, every cat in town is going to be grateful to us. We'll be the Sherlock Holmes and Dr Watson of this place!"

"Who?" asked Dog, puzzled.

"Sherlock Holmes and Dr Watson," said Cat.

"Are they a dog and a cat?"

"No, they were famous human detectives. They solved every case they took on."

"Did they have a case of disappearing fish?" asked Dog.

"No," said Cat, getting slightly impatient. "They were just very clever. Well, Sherlock Holmes was. He was the clever one."

"So am I Sherlock Holmes?" asked Dog, brightly.

Cat hesitated.

"Yes," she said with a sigh. "You're Sherlock Holmes."

"Great!" said Dog. "Then we'd better go and solve this case, Watson!" He frowned. "How do we start?"

"We go to a fish shop and see if anyone steals the fish from it. Then we follow them and find out what they're up to."

"Yes," agreed Dog. "That's what I was about to say. Let's go!"

Chapter 2
Follow the Rats

Cat and Dog watched the back of the fish shop. They had been waiting there for an hour. In that time nothing had happened, except that Dog had found some tasty food in a dustbin: half a cheese sandwich, a meat pie and the remains of some potato salad.

"Gross!" said Cat as she watched Dog eat.

"Tasty!" smiled Dog, munching.

Suddenly, Cat spotted seven rats coming out of the back of the fish shop. They were wobbling under the weight of a wooden box loaded with fish.

"We've got them!" said Cat excitedly.

Dog swallowed the rest of the meat pie in one gulp.

"Do we arrest them?" he asked.

"No," said Cat. "We follow them and find out where they're taking the fish."

Cat and Dog hid behind the dustbins. The rats struggled past, just about managing to carry the box of fish.

"Why do we have to keep doing this?" groaned one of the rats.

"We've got to keep The Big One happy," said another. "Come on!"

The rats wobbled off and disappeared around a corner.

"Who is this Big One?" Dog wondered.

"It's what crooks call the top gangster," said Cat. "We'd better track him down."

Dog frowned.

"Isn't that dangerous?" he asked.

"Possibly," said Cat. "But we're detectives. We laugh at danger."

Dog frowned.

"Why do we do that?" he asked.

Cat shook her head.

"I don't know," she said. "It's what brave detectives do. Anyway, we'd better follow those rats."

Cat and Dog hurried after the rats, but when they looked around the corner, there was no sign of either the rats or the fish.

"They've vanished!" said Cat.

"Leave this to me," said Dog.

He put his nose to the pavement and began to follow the scent, sniffing hard as he ran. He stopped at a manhole cover.

"They went down here," he said.

Cat and Dog lifted the manhole cover. A bad smell rose up out of the hole.

"Pooh! What a dreadful smell!" said Cat, wrinkling her nose.

"It's a sewer," said Dog. "Sewers smell like that."

He moved forward to look down the hole, and as he did so he knocked against Cat, who tumbled down into the sewer below.

"Aaaargh!" shouted Cat.

There was a splash.

"I'll save you!" called Dog.

He leaped down into the hole and landed on top of Cat. Her head was just popping up out of the foul-smelling water, but Dog knocked her back under again.

"Yuk!" said Cat, coming back to the surface.

She pulled herself on to a narrow ledge in the sewer that ran beside the water channel. Dog climbed out after her on to the ledge.

"That tastes disgusting!" said Cat, spitting out a mouthful of the water.

"It's not too bad," said Dog. "I've tasted worse."

Cat looked along the sewer.

"Which way did they go?" she asked.

"Follow the nose!" said Dog. And he began to move along the ledge, sniffing as he went.

Chapter 3
The Big One

Dog ran through the sewer with Cat following. The smell of fish was getting stronger all the time.

"That's not just the smell of fresh fish," said Cat. "*That* is the smell of fish that have gone rotten."

Suddenly Dog stopped.

"I can hear claws," he said. "The rats are coming back! We have to hide!"

"Where?" asked Cat. "There's nowhere!"

"There's one place," said Dog.

With that, Dog grabbed Cat and jumped off the ledge into the dirty water of the sewer. Cat struggled, but Dog held her until he was sure the rats had gone past.

"There!" he said, as they bobbed back to the surface.

Cat spat out another mouthful of water as she climbed back on to the ledge. They could see the rats disappearing around a corner.

"That wasn't funny!" snorted Cat.

Dog sniffed.

"The smell of rotten fish is getting worse," he said. "Can't you smell it?"

"No," said Cat sourly. "Because of the water in my nose."

Dog set off along the sewer ledge. The sewer came to a bend, and as Dog went around the bend, he stopped suddenly, causing Cat to bash into him.

"Wow!" he said.

"What?" asked Cat.

She joined Dog and looked around the bend. There, where three tunnels met, an enormous pile of fish loomed out of the water. It was a huge mountain of fish, reaching right up and almost touching the ceiling of the sewer.

"Yuk!" said Cat, putting a paw over her nose. "That is the worst smell I've ever smelled!"

Suddenly they heard the scamper of rats' claws coming from a different direction. They looked around the corner and peered out. Another lot of rats were coming from another part of the sewer. They were also struggling under the weight of more fish. They added these fish to the huge pile, then disappeared back the way they'd come.

"What are the rats up to?" asked Dog. "Why would The Big One make them do this?"

"Let's go and take a look at the fish and maybe we'll find out," said Cat.

They moved forward and approached the mountain of fish. The smell was so powerful it brought tears to their eyes.

"I'm going to call this *The Case of the Big Stink*," said Cat, still holding her nose.

They stood and studied the pile. It was just fish. There was nothing else there.

"Maybe there's something precious hidden inside the fish," said Cat.

"What kind of thing?" asked Dog.

"Who knows," said Cat. "Gold? Money? Jewels?"

"Why would anyone put things like that inside a pile of fish?" asked Dog.

"To stop people finding them," said Cat. "No one would want to start digging into that lot."

"So how can we find out if there is anything precious hidden in there?" asked Dog.

Cat studied the stinking pile.

"There's only one way," she said. "You have to go into it."

Dog looked at the pile of fish.

"Why me?" he asked.

"Because you're a detective," said Cat.

"So are you," said Dog.

"Yes, but I've got a sensitive nose," said Cat.

"My nose is more sensitive than yours," said Dog. "That's why dogs can follow smells like we do."

Cat looked unhappily at the pile of fish.

"If only we knew who this mysterious Big One was, we'd know what all this is about," she said.

Suddenly, there was the sound of a growl behind them. A deep growl that made the fur on the back of their necks stand up.

Slowly, they turned, and came face-to-face with the biggest animal they'd ever seen. An enormous brown bear. Cat looked at its powerful arms and sharp claws. As the bear opened its huge mouth, she also noticed its very, very sharp teeth.

Chapter 4
Escape by Smell

The bear let out a terrifying roar.

"Help!" squeaked Cat. "Someone save us!"

The bear looked around, puzzled.

"Save you from what?" he asked.

"Er ... from you," said Cat.

"Why?" asked the bear.

"Aren't you dangerous?" asked Dog.

"No," said the bear.

"But you roared."

"That's because I'm so unhappy."

"Why?" asked Cat.

"I suppose it's my fault," said the bear gloomily. And he told them his story.

"I used to be in a small private zoo, but I was lonely because I was the only bear there. One day, the owner left my cage door unlocked and I managed to sneak off. But being in the city scared me, so I hid in the sewers. Then I got hungry, and there was no food for me down here."

"The rats took pity on me. They asked me what I liked eating, and I said fish, so they spread the word among all the rats in the city to bring fish for me."

He pointed unhappily at the pile. "And that's what happened. More fish than I can ever eat!" He gave a sad sigh. "The trouble is, the rats have been so kind that I don't like to hurt their feelings by telling them to stop. But I don't want to be in this sewer any more. I want to go somewhere else, somewhere I can see daylight."

Dog looked at Cat.

"You said this is what detectives do," he said. "Solve problems. And this bear has got a big problem that needs to be solved."

"Yes," nodded Cat thoughtfully.

She fell into a deep silence, looking at the bear, and at the huge pile of fish, then back at the bear again.

"What's she doing?" asked the bear anxiously.

"She's thinking," said Dog. "Usually I do the thinking, because I'm the clever one, but today it's her turn."

"I've got it!" exclaimed Cat. "Just outside town there's a Wild Animal Park. There are no cages. The people who come to see them drive around in cars, and the animals can just wander where they like. And they've got bears at this Wild Animal Park. If you went to live there, you wouldn't be lonely."

"It sounds wonderful!" said the bear happily. Then he looked sad again. "But how can I get there without being spotted? If anyone sees me, they'll report me and I'll be taken back to my old zoo."

"Leave that to us! We have a plan!" announced Cat.

"You do?" exclaimed the bear. "What is it?" And he looked at Dog.

"Er …" said Dog. He pointed at Cat. "I'll let her explain."

"There's an animal supplies shop in the centre of town," said Cat. "A truck from the Wild Animal Park picks up food there every afternoon. We wait for the truck to make its collection, then climb on board and hide in the back of it."

"But how do we get to this shop without me being seen?" sighed the bear unhappily.

"Through the sewers," said Cat. "There's a manhole in the street at the back of the shop, right near where the truck parks."

The bear gaped at her.

"That's brilliant!" he said.

"Yes, it is," agreed Dog. "We have good ideas. That's because we're detectives with good thinking brains."

The bear looked at the three tunnels that led away from the pile of fish.

"So, which tunnel do we take to get to this shop?" he asked.

Cat frowned. "Actually, I'm not sure," she admitted. Then she smiled. "But right next to the shop are a load of takeaway food shops: a curry restaurant, a kebab shop, a pizza place and a fish and chip shop." She looked at Dog. "How good is your nose? Could you smell your way to them?"

"To that lot?" said Dog. "No problem!"

"Right, so let's go," said Cat. "If my calculations are right, the truck will be arriving at the shop very soon."

Chapter 5
Spotted!

They were just heading off down one of the sewer's tunnels when they heard the familiar sound of rats approaching. A team of rats staggered around the bend in the sewer, holding a wooden box loaded with fish.

"Here you are, Big One!" panted one of the rats as they dropped the box by the huge pile of fish. "More fish for you!"

"Thank you," said Cat, "but there'll be no need for you to keep bringing fish for the bear."

"I'm moving to a new home," said the bear. "One where I'll have other bears for company, and get lots to eat."

"Hurray!" shouted the rats with relief. "That's wonderful news!"

"I want you to know how grateful I am to you rats for all the hard work you've done for me," said the bear. "It's meant so much to me."

"It was our pleasure," said a rat.

"We'd better hurry if we're going to catch that truck," said Cat.

The rats waved goodbye as Cat and the bear followed Dog into one of the tunnels.

Dog hurried along, sniffing the air as he ran.

"I'm smelling pizza and kebab," he said. "And curry." He ran on a bit further, then announced, "And there's definitely fish and chips! We're getting near!"

Cat and the bear followed Dog until he stopped beneath a manhole.

"This is it," he told them. He looked up at the manhole cover and frowned. "The trouble is, it's too high for us to reach to open it."

"Not for me," said the huge bear. He reached up and pushed the manhole cover upwards; then he lifted Dog and pushed him up through the hole. A second later, Cat was lifted up and pushed through the manhole to join Dog. Then the bear squeezed out to join them.

The bear was just putting the manhole cover back in place, when a little boy appeared from the animal supplies shop. He stared at them in amazement.

"Bear!" shouted the boy.

"Quick! Hide!" shouted Cat.

Cat grabbed hold of the bear's paw and hauled him behind some dustbins. Dog stood, shocked, unsure what to do.

The boy's mother had come out of the shop at her son's yell.

"What?" she asked.

The boy pointed towards the dustbins.

"There's a bear over there!" he shouted.

His mother glared at him.

"Really, Tommy! Your imagination will get you in trouble. That's just a dog."

Immediately, Dog nodded and let out a bark.

"No!" shouted Tommy. "It's by the dustbins!"

Dog walked over to the dustbins and stood beside them.

"Yes, I can see it," snapped Tommy's mother. "And I can also see it's a dog. Now stop making things up or you won't have any cake when we get home."

She grabbed the boy by the hand and walked off with him.

When the woman and Tommy had gone, Cat and the bear crept out of hiding. Cat pointed to where a large truck was parked. On the side was painted 'Wild Animal Park'.

"That's the one," she said.

But just as she said it, the truck started up.

"Oh no!" she said. "It's picked up the supplies and now it's going! We're too late!"

Chapter 6
Home at Last

Suddenly Dog rushed towards the truck, barking loudly. As he jumped in front of it, still barking, the truck pulled to a stop.

"Quick!" shouted Cat.

She ran to the back of the truck, jumped up and hung on to the door handle, making the rear door swing open.

The bear jumped inside, followed by Cat.

There was the sound of the truck hooting its horn, and Dog stopped barking. As the truck began to roll forward, Dog ran to the back and jumped in to join Cat and the bear.

Cat pulled the back door shut as the truck moved off.

"That was quick thinking, Dog," said Cat. "You *are* clever."

"So are you, Cat," said Dog.

"You two make a good team," said the bear.

The three sat in the back of the truck as it rolled along. After it had been driving for what seemed like ages, it stopped.

"Are we there?" asked the bear.

"I don't know," said Cat. "It might have stopped for more supplies."

"No," said Dog. "We're there." He sniffed. "I can smell lions and tigers and camels and giraffes."

"And bears?" asked the bear.

"And bears," nodded Dog.

They heard the door of the driver's cab open, then shut, then footsteps walking away.

"Right," said Cat. "Let's go."

Carefully, she opened the door and peered out. They were in the car park beside the back door of the Wild Animal Park.

"This is it," she whispered. "Out you come."

The three of them got out. There was a high wire fence running all the way around the Park. Too high for them to climb over. The back entrance was locked.

"How do we get in?" asked the bear.

"We ring the bell," said Cat.

She went to a bell beside the door which said 'Staff Only'. She jumped up and jabbed at the bell, before dropping back to the ground.

"You stay here," she said to the bear. "We've got to hide," she told Dog.

Cat and Dog went behind the truck and watched and waited.

After a while, they saw a woman in green overalls approach the door from inside the fence. She stopped in shock when she opened the door and saw the bear outside.

"Ted! Dawn! There's a bear here!" she shouted.

A man and a woman, also wearing green overalls, came running. They all stared at the bear.

"Is it one of ours?" asked Dawn.

"What's it doing?" asked Ted.

"Waiting to come in, by the look of it," said the woman.

"Well, let it in! Quick!" said Dawn.

"It doesn't look like one of our bears," said Ted.

"It doesn't matter. We can't have a lost bear wandering around," said Dawn.

She unlocked the gate. "In you come," she said to the bear.

The bear walked through the gate into the Wild Animal Park.

"Let's take you to the other bears," said Dawn. "Follow me."

The bear turned and waved goodbye to Cat and Dog, and then followed Dawn.

"And the bear lived happily ever after," said Cat.

"That sounds like a story," said Dog.

"It is," said Cat. "And this one has a happy ending."

"Not completely happy," said Dog.

"What do you mean?" asked Cat.

"How far is it back to home?" Dog asked.

"About five miles," said Cat.

"And we have to walk all the way," said Dog.

"Yes," nodded Cat. "Good point." She sighed. "I suppose we'd better start walking."

About the author

I've been writing for many years, and have had 100 books published and 500 TV and radio scripts broadcast. My inspiration to write started when I was very young: at the age of six I was hospitalized for about a year with a serious illness, and spent most of that year in bed. In those days there were no televisions in hospitals, and so my entertainment was reading and listening to drama and comedy on the radio. I grew up thinking "I'd love to write books and scripts one day". Which is why, today, I'm able to present you with *The Big Stink*. I do hope you enjoy it!